That Is Too High to Fly!

(Afraid of Heights)

WHY SO SCARED: BOOK ONE

Heath DeLany

ISBN 979-8-88616-137-3 (hardcover)
ISBN 979-8-88616-138-0 (digital)

Christian Faith Publishing
832 Park Avenue
Meadville, PA 16335
www.christianfaithpublishing.com

Printed in the United States of America

To my daughters, who did not hesitate to soar; to my grandkids, who never stop trying to take off; and to TeriAnn, who showed me the sky is a goal, not a limit. You all inspire me every day.

In a Kansas field of waving amber-colored grass stood a tree that Percy called home. Percy was a possum who enjoyed being friends with everyone. As the sun came up over the horizon, Percy was preparing to go to bed after a long night of foraging.

Just before he went into his home for the day, he noticed a bluebird flying by. The blue jay was flying no more than two feet above the ground.

Percy, being the friendly individual he was, yelled "Hello!" to the passing blue jay. The blue jay glanced back with a puzzled look on his face but said nothing to Percy and continued on his way.

Percy noticed the blue jay a couple of times over the next few days. Every day Percy said hi, but every day the blue jay ignored Percy's friendly gesture. Percy was not one to give up easily and never got tired of being friendly. On the fifth day, after Percy said hello, the blue jay circled back around and landed at the base of the tree where Percy stood.

The blue jay asked Percy, "Why are you talking to me? We are so different, and we have nothing in common!"

Percy told the blue jay, "I like to be friends with everyone, and I am always polite. Since I have never seen you before, I wanted to say hi and introduce myself."

Percy said, "My name is Percy, and I'm a possum. What is your name?"

The blue jay looked puzzled as he told Percy his name. "I'm Jackson, and I'm a blue jay."

Jackson told Percy he did not need any more friends, especially friends who look so different.

Percy explained to Jackson, "Friendship does not stop at a person's status or looks. If you pick your friends by the way they look, you may lose out on a great friendship. Just because people look the same does not mean they will always get along. The same as when people look different, it does not mean they have to be enemies. I have friends that look like me, I have friends that look like you, and I have friends that do not look like either one of us. You should allow a person's character to decide if they can be a friend, not the way they look."

Jackson agreed with Percy's point of view. He liked the thought of being able to have friends who do not look like him and asked Percy how he does it.

Percy told Jackson, "I do it the same way I got you to stop and talk to me. People will not let you have fun by yourself, and people always want to have a friendly conversation."

Percy told Jackson, "Some people are afraid to start a conversation in fear of being embarrassed if the person ignores them."

Percy said, "Once a person sees that you care enough to ask them about their day, most people will open up and be friendly. Being kind to each other and sharing kind words help us understand each other's struggles in life."

A look of understanding came over Jackson's face. Percy's explanation helped Jackson see that you do not have to surround yourself with similar-looking people to have friends. Jackson agreed that he and Percy could be friends, after all. Jackson recognized that Percy took the time and effort to make a connection. Jackson did not want to be rude and decided a person can never have too many friends. Jackson thanked Percy for teaching him how friends come in all shapes, sizes, and colors. Jackson told Percy to have a good day and told Percy he would see him tomorrow.

As Jackson flew away, Percy noticed Jackson still did not fly too far off the ground. Percy did not understand why and struggled with whether he wanted to bring it up to Jackson or not. New friendships can be fragile, but friendships need honesty. If you have a good friend, you should be able to have discussions about difficult topics.

Over the course of the next week, Percy waved and said hello to Jackson, and Jackson would acknowledge Percy with a simple "Hello" or "Good morning." Percy kept noticing that Jackson never flew too high off the ground. This puzzled Percy and made him more curious as to why a bird, who can fly as high as he wants, never flies more than a few feet off the ground.

One day, Percy decided he had to know why Jackson flew so close to the ground. Instead of the usual hello, Percy hollered at Jackson and asked him to please come back and talk with him.

Jackson, looking annoyed, flew back to Percy's home. Landing at the base of the tree, Jackson asked Percy, "What do you want now?"

Percy asked Jackson if he could ask him a question.

Jackson said, "Of course you can. After all, we are friends."

Percy told Jackson he noticed Jackson never flew more than a couple of feet off the ground. Percy asked Jackson why he doesn't fly into the trees like the other birds.

Jackson seemed annoyed and upset that Percy would ask him that question. Jackson told Percy that he was a possum and did not understand anything about birds. Jackson told Percy that he did not have to explain why he doesn't fly high and that it was none of Percy's business. Jackson flew off, angry that Percy would even ask him that question. Percy felt bad about upsetting Jackson but still noticed Jackson did not fly too far off the ground.

The two fell back into the same routine of saying hi without any other interaction for a week. Percy was afraid he had upset Jackson and Jackson would not want to be his friend. Percy was determined not to lose his friend and never stopped saying hi to Jackson every morning.

Finally, after seven days of only saying hi, Jackson circled back around to speak with Percy. Percy was happy that his friend had decided to speak to him. Percy apologized for asking about the flying thing. Percy told Jackson that he has always been able to talk to a friend about anything, so he thought it would be okay to ask about Jackson's flying habits.

Jackson apologized for getting upset. Jackson told Percy that he felt embarrassed and realized that Percy did not intend to make him mad. The two smiled and went into Percy's house for tea.

As Percy and Jackson sat at the table, enjoying their tea, Jackson got quiet and looked sad.

Percy asked Jackson, "What's wrong?"

Jackson told Percy that he did not want to tell him because he would laugh. Percy told Jackson that he was a friend and that Jackson's problems were his problems as well. If Percy laughed, he would be laughing at himself.

Jackson took a deep breath and told Percy, "I am afraid of heights." Jackson said this in a low mumbled tone, so Percy had to ask, "What did you say?"

Jackson, almost yelling this time, said, "I'm afraid of heights!"

Percy's jaw dropped open, and a smile started across his face, but he stopped himself from laughing. With a look of amazement, Percy asked the question in disbelief, "You are afraid of heights!"

Jackson, now with an angry look on his face, said, "Yes!"

Percy composed his look of amusement to explain that he was not laughing at Jackson; he was surprised at the news. Percy told Jackson it was not every day one met a bird who was afraid of heights.

Percy told Jackson, "Friends will laugh at a problem, but only because they know they are going to help overcome the issue. Laughter helps bridge the gap into a solution."

Percy told Jackson, "I am your friend, and there is no tree we can't climb together—literally."

A look of relief came over Jackson, and he was able to smile.

Jackson asked Percy, "You really think you can help me?"

Percy said, "We will give it a shot. If we cannot get you past your fear, at least I will be there with you."

Jackson thanked Percy for being his friend and asked for more tea.

Percy and Jackson sat drinking tea and talking while learning about each other. Percy asked Jackson why he feared heights. Jackson explained that when he was a baby bird, his mother flew off one day for food and did not come home. Jackson said he got hungry and followed a caterpillar out onto a branch.

The caterpillar went into a hole, and Jackson slipped. He fell from the branch, striking other branches as he fell. Jackson said he wound up on the ground with a hurt leg. Jackson told Percy that as his leg healed, he lived in a knot at the base of the tree. Jackson practiced flying but never wanted to get hurt again, so he never flew back into the tree. Jackson's injury healed, but he never got over the feeling of failure when he fell to the ground.

Percy told Jackson the fear could be overcome but that it would take trust and patience. Percy said he would help and have Jackson up in the trees in no time. Percy then yawned and said they would have to start tomorrow. Percy said he was so tired from a long night of foraging and needed to get some sleep. Jackson understood and went on about his day so his friend could get some sleep.

The next morning, Percy and Jackson met up in front of Percy's house. The tall tree Percy lived under would be the perfect starting point for Jackson's new self-challenge. Jackson asked Percy if he was able to sleep after he left. Percy told Jackson he did and was ready for the day.

Percy told Jackson, "In order to overcome a fear, you must face it. Until you confront what scares you, the thing that scares you has control. Let's start by climbing this tree. We do not have to go to the top. Let's start on the lower branches."

Percy climbed to a branch about four feet off the ground and told Jackson to join him. Jackson looked hesitant to even try and get to Percy. Jackson flapped his wings, flew halfway to Percy, and returned to the ground.

Percy told Jackson, "You have to own the fear and not let the fear own you."

Jackson took a deep breath, looked up at Percy, and flapped his wings. This time, Jackson made it to the branch where Percy waited. As Jackson tried to land on the branch, he missed and fell to the ground. Percy climbed down to comfort his friend, who was now sitting on the ground with a disappointed look on his face.

Percy told Jackson, "You were there, what happened?"

Jackson said that all he could think about was the fall that happened when he was young. Jackson did not want to get hurt again. Percy patted his friend on the shoulder and said he understood. Percy told Jackson that it was all right to be afraid, it is even okay to fail, but it is never okay to give in to fear of failure and never try.

Percy reminded Jackson that he has wings. "Jackson," Percy said, "you can not only fly, but you can glide. If you fall off the branch, extend your wings and glide to the ground."

Percy said that he was not that fortunate and fell several times when learning to climb trees. "Now, let's try this again."

Percy climbed the tree to the same spot he was the first time. Percy asked Jackson, "Are you ready to give it another try?"

Jackson, with a newfound sense of determination, stood up, took a deep breath, and flew to his friend in the tree. Jackson landed on the branch, almost fell but was able to catch his balance. Jackson was now in a tree for the first time since he fell out of one.

Excited for his friend, Percy jumped up and down, cheering for Jackson. The branch shook, and Jackson lost his grip. Jackson fell from the branch. As Jackson fell, he remembered he has wings. As he fell, Jackson extended his wings and softly landed on the ground.

Jackson looked up at Percy, who was still jumping up and down. Jackson had a big smile on his face and knew he had taken a big step. Percy lost his balance and fell from the tree. Percy hit the ground and was still laughing with excitement for his friend. Jackson asked Percy if he was okay.

Percy told Jackson, "I am better than okay. I am over the moon for my friend's accomplishment."

Jackson said, "But you fell from the tree."

Percy said, "That is not my first fall, and it will not be my last. This moment belongs to you, Jackson."

HA HA HA
J

Percy asked if Jackson wanted to go to another branch. Jackson told Percy he would like that very much. Percy started climbing the tree and said, "I bet I can beat you to the branch in the middle of the tree!"

Jackson said, "You're on!" he flapped his wings.

The two friends made it to the branch at the same time. They laughed together as Percy congratulated Jackson on the huge accomplishment. Jackson told Percy that he could never have done it without him.

Percy told Jackson, "You did it. All I did was remind you of your inner strength. You faced your fear and beat it."

Jackson told Percy that he still has not flown more than a couple of feet off the ground.

Percy said, "Well, there is no time like the present for new things."

Percy asked Jackson if he thought he could make it to the tree across the field. Jackson asked if Percy wanted to race. Percy said not this time because Jackson would have too much of an advantage.

Percy said, "I would have to climb down this tree, run across the field, and climb up the other tree. You only need to soar to the branch and back. I will wait here."

Jackson took a deep breath and flapped his wings as he leaped from the branch. Jackson glided nervously to the tree and landed on a branch of the same height. With excitement about his accomplishment, Jackson let out a few chirps. "*Chirp, chirp, chirp.*" Jackson then repeated the steps and returned to the tree where Percy waited.

Percy congratulated Jackson for the big steps he had taken today.

Jackson took a deep breath and let out a song of excitement. "*Chirp-chirp-chirp-whistle-whistle-chirp-chirp-chirp!*"

Percy smiled and told Jackson that he loved the song and hoped he got to hear it more often.

Jackson told Percy, "I have not felt like singing in a long time. Thank you for helping me, believe in me."

Percy told Jackson, "That is what a friend does."

Percy yawned and told Jackson it was time for bed. If he didn't mind, he would leave Jackson to practice going from tree to tree on his own. Jackson told Percy he would be okay working on his own and told Percy to sleep well as he flew toward the other tree.

The next day, Percy was concerned when he did not see Jackson fly past his house. Percy thought something may have happened to his friend. As Percy stood there in front of his home, high in the tree above him, he heard a triumphant song: the *chirp-chirp-chirp-whistle-whistle-chirp-chirp-chirp* he remembered from Jackson yesterday.

Percy looked up to see Jackson singing in the tree above his home. Jackson was not on the middle branch, though; Jackson was now on the branch near the top of the tree.

Percy climbed the tree to where Jackson stood singing. Percy waited for Jackson to finish the song before saying good morning. Jackson finished his song, but before Percy could say anything, Jackson said, "Gooood morning, Percy!"

Jackson looked happier than Percy has ever seen him. Seeing Jackson this happy made Percy happy for his friend. Percy said, "Good morning, Jackson."

Jackson told Percy he hoped his night went well.

Jackson said, "After you went to sleep yesterday, I don't think my feet touched the ground."

Jackson said he flew from tree to tree and telephone pole to telephone pole until the sun went down. Jackson said he now understood that fears are real but overcoming them takes away their control. Percy told Jackson he was proud of his accomplishment and hoped he got to hear his song for many years to come.

Jackson flew off, saying, "You can! The only thing now is you will have to listen up!"

The End

About the Author

Heath DeLany was born and raised in Houston, Texas. His father, Lawrence DeLany, was a law enforcement officer there. He is the reason Heath got into law enforcement. Heath became a sheriff's deputy in Jackson County, Kansas, and fell in love with serving his community.

He has a master's degree in criminal justice and jail administration and spent several years singing in a band. He hopes this book opens the readers' minds to understand that fear can be conquered.